SCOTLAND TRAVEL GUIDE 2023

THE COMPLETE GUIDE TO SCOTLAND'S MOST BEAUTIFUL SIGHTS | DISCOVER ANCIENT HISTORY, ART, ATTRACTIONS, CULTURE AND DELICIOUS FOODS UNMISSABLE ON YOUR NEXT TRIP

BY

MIKE J. DARCEY

Scotland, UK

Orkney Islands

North Atlantic Ocean

Na h-Eileanan Siar

Highland

Moray

Aberdeenshire

Aberdeen City

Angus

Perth and Kinross

Argyll and Bute

Stirling

Fife

4

North Sea

1. Glasgow City
2. East Dunbartonshire
3. West Dunbartonshire
4. Dundee City
5. Inverclyde
6. Clackmannanshire
7. North Lanarkshire
8. West Lothian
9. Midlothian
10. Renfrewshire
11. East Renfrewshire
12. Falkirk
13. Edinburgh

6

3 2 12

5 10   7   8   13

11   9

East Lothian

North Ayrshire

South Lanarkshire

Scottish Borders

East Ayrshire

South Ayrshire

Dumfries and Galloway

IRELAND

Northern Ireland

Isle of Man

England

Table of Contents

Introduction

This Introduction travel guide will help you plan your trip and give you a great insight into what Scotland has to offer.

It is known for its mountains, rolling hills, wild craggy castles and its fresh water lochs. Scottish history is interesting and varied, from its ancient Gaelic culture to the re-emergence of Roman Catholicism.

Besides its rich history, Scotland has a distinctive accent that varies greatly from one region to the next. Its language, Scots, is considered to be the oldest of the British languages and is used by over 7 million people.

There is also freedom to roam in Scotland, which means you are free to walk along the countryside and inland water. This is a great way to enjoy the natural environment and wildlife. But be aware that some areas are protected by law and you should not trespass on private property.

The Highlands

The Highlands are the most mountainous, scenic and romantic area of Scotland. Home to breathtaking lochs and rugged mountains, this region is perfect for hiking and cycling, with a vast array of activities available.

The landscape here is dominated by high mountain summits and a rugged coastline, where white peaks disappear in the horizon, and wildlife thrives in the wild. A journey to the Scottish Highlands is a must for anyone looking for an unforgettable experience of nature and history.

Aside from being a beautiful place to visit, the Highlands also offer many fascinating facts about its history. These claims were met with fierce resistance from local residents. The resulting battles, massacres and bloodsheds were a part of the Highlands' dark history.

The region is home to some of the country's most beautiful and historic castles, and there are many tours that depart from Inverness.

Travelling to the Highlands can be a bit daunting, so it's a good idea to take some precautions.

The Lowlands

The area is divided by a number of major hills, many of which are volcanic in origin.

The Lowland region is characterized by a diverse cultural and economic practice, ranging from the industrial cities of Glasgow and Edinburgh to rural farming areas and small towns. Generally speaking, the regions within the Lowlands are considered to be more rural than the Highlands.

In the past, the Lowlands were largely populated by people who spoke Scots or English while the Highlands were inhabited by Gaelic speakers. However, since the 17th century this has changed.

As a result, the two regions have diverged culturally. Those who live in the Lowlands speak a variant form of English called Lowland Scots, while those who live in the Highlands are more likely to speak Gaelic.

It was this cultural and linguistic difference that caused Scotland to become a separate country from England in 1707, when the Scottish parliament passed the Act of Union. It also caused the Scots language to be regarded as its own language, rather than an English dialect. This led to a great deal of trouble in the past, including the so-called Highland Clearances.

The Islands

Islands are an essential part of a Scotland trip and can offer visitors a unique way to experience the country. But they are also a diverse collection of places and are best explored by choosing carefully.

The National Islands Plan focuses on how Scotland can improve the lives of people living in its islands, with particular attention paid to reducing isolation and increasing their resilience and well-being. There is a wealth of community-led initiatives that are already taking place to support these objectives. These include green recovery programmes, low carbon transportation, zero waste projects and food sustainability funding schemes.

Edinburgh

Drapped across a series of rocky hills that overlook the sea, the city is dotted with monuments and buildings that tower over the cliffs, and it's all framed by a breathtaking landscape.

But what's most special about this town is that it has a real, down-to-earth charm that's hard to find elsewhere in the world. Its narrow and cobbled passageways (called closes in Scots) are a perfect contrast to the bustle of the main streets, which makes it the ideal city for exploring on foot.

Aside from being the home of countless fascinating museums, it also boasts many historical landmarks that are worth visiting. The UNESCO-listed Old Town, for example, is a jumble of medieval tenements that rise high along the Royal Mile, and it's a wonderful place to explore on foot.

Glasgow

Glasgow, a city known worldwide for its innovation and creativity, is an exciting place to explore. It's a great place to visit if you're looking for a fun and lively atmosphere, with friendly people who are always ready to have a good time.

The city's history is a fascinating mix of ancient and modern, with historic buildings lining the streets of the city centre that have survived for centuries. In the 18th century, it became an international trade hub and was one of the world's biggest shipyards during the Industrial Revolution.

With a rich cultural heritage and many important public buildings, Glasgow is an exciting city for anyone to explore. Its vibrant contemporary arts, music and architecture scene is renowned around the world.

For those who love cinema, the Glasgow Film Theatre is a must-visit. It has a fantastic selection of films, from the classics to contemporary art house movies.

Those visiting the city will also be interested in its thriving experimental music scene, which plays host to many of the UK's best underground DJs. There are a number of venues and record labels that cater to this style of music, including Sub Club, Arches and the Soma label.

The Isles

The British Isles were formed by tectonic movements and exposure to glaciations over millions of years. Currently, the British Isles consist of the United Kingdom (which includes Scotland, England and Wales) and the Republic of Ireland.

Several tectonic plates collided over time to form mountains in Ireland and Scotland, with some of the islands becoming exposed to ocean ice. These icebergs eventually dissolved, creating the islands we see today.

There is a long history of settlement by different peoples in the islands, and they became part of a network of Celtic kingdoms that stretched from England in the south to the Irish coast in the north. Their influence extended beyond the island of Scotland, and they were eventually ruled by Vikings from Norway.

A particularly notable figure in the history of the Western Isles was Somerled, who challenged the might of both Scotland and Norway to make the islands an independent kingdom that answered only to him. Somerled was born around 1117 and had a mixed Norse and Gaelic pedigree.

Chapter 1.

Brief historical overview of

Scotland.

For thousands of years, tribes lived in Scotland, building stone huts and hunting wild animals. Little remains of this era today, but the stone circles at Stenness and Callanish are reminders of these early societies. However, in Caledonia, or Scotland, they faced resistance from a tribe known as the Picts. Rome built a wall called Hadrian's Wall to try and keep the tribes out.

Romans

The arrival of the Romans in Scotland was not an easy one. For centuries, the country was dominated by dispersed tribes who were prone to fierce rivalries.

However, the arrival of Rome brought these disparate groups together in a fight against a common enemy.

Despite this, there was an occasional presence of Roman troops in Scotland during the early and middle centuries of the first millennium AD. But even then they didn't really hold any territory for long.

The Romans eventually withdrew south of Hadrian's Wall, leaving the northern frontier at the Solway-Tyne isthmus as the limit of their power in Britain. They also abandoned most of their forts in southern Scotland around 105AD. The presence of Roman legions in Scotland may have been necessary to suppress rebellions elsewhere in the empire, but there's little evidence that it had a significant impact on Scottish history.

Vikings

Over the course of hundreds of years, the Vikings shaped Scotland. Their raids and settlements made a huge impact on the country's history.

The Vikings first arrived in Scotland during the 8th century. They initially settled in Shetland and Orkney, as well as Caithness and the Hebrides.

These settlements were useful for them because they allowed them to raid areas on the mainland of Scotland and the Western Isles.

Edward I

A shrewd and realistic king, Edward understood that his success depended on the support of his barons. To this end, he made a series of important reforms that aimed to protect the rights of barons and increase their control over local administration.

He also acted to protect his home base of England and to build the foundations for a successful future. In addition, he used parliaments to increase his power and gain support from the people. These meetings were usually composed of representatives of shires, boroughs and the lesser clergy.

William Wallace

One of Scotland's most famous national heroes, William Wallace led his people on a noble quest to freedom from English oppression. Immortalised in Mel Gibson's Braveheart, his impact on the history of Scotland is still felt to this day.

Most historians agree that Wallace was born around 1272, but the exact details are not clear. Some say he was the youngest son of a landholder; others believe he fought as a mercenary in the wars waged by Edward I of England, so must have had some military experience.

During the conflict, Wallace travelled north into northern England to lead an attack on the English army. His plan was to show Edward that if he pressed south, Scotland could also take the battle back into its own territory and inflict damage on Edward's forces.

On September 11, 1297, Wallace's army attacked the English at Stirling Bridge - a narrow bridge crossing the River Forth – and forced them to retreat. Wallace's strategy won him a decisive victory and earned him the title of Guardian of Scotland.

Highland Clearances

The Highland Clearances were a period in the history of Scotland where many people were dispossessed of their land. This forced them to move to other parts of Scotland or emigrate overseas, where they could start a new life.

Before the Clearances, Scottish clans had a strong system of family and fealty. They had land in the Highlands and were owned by the clan chief, who would rent it to poorer members of the family through a tacksman (the person who leased land from a clan chief).

The tacksmen were a key part of highland society and were very important in maintaining family relations and culture. But after the Highland Clearances, the system of clanship fell apart, and the tacksmen were no longer needed. Instead, they were forced to sell their lands and move to the coasts to work in kelping or fishing industries. These were booming trades at the time, and they were considered more financially profitable than farming sheep.

Age of Enlightenment

In the 18th century, Scotland played a major role in the Age of Enlightenment. This was a period of intellectual ferment in which numerous breakthroughs in philosophy, ethics, history, jurisprudence, sociology and political science were made.

The Enlightenment was a hugely important period in Scotland's history as it brought about significant improvements in the country's society and economy. The economic theories of Adam Smith were influential in the development of modern business and the invention of the steam engine had a dramatic impact on the growth of industry.

Industrial Revolution

By the early 19th century Scotland was a large, rich country with huge mining and iron-smelting industries. The population increased dramatically and Scotland was one of Europe's most urbanized societies.

This rapid growth of industry, while bringing work and wealth, imposed severe pressure on the poor and working classes.

The Industrial Revolution was not without its critics, including the so-called Luddites. But in the end, the Industrial Revolution transformed Scotland, creating a modern country.

The Second World War

It triggered huge anxiety, suffering and loss, and it affected the country's population on both a personal and national level.

Children were evacuated from towns and cities, with some settling in foster homes to help them adjust to life away from home. The war also affected the country's economy, with factories closing and industries being restructured.

A number of important defence measures were made, such as the strengthening of the north-east coast and the installation of coastal batteries in Orkney.

Scottish Independence

Scotland has a long history of extraordinary growth and change. The important event in Scotland's history was the struggle for independence. In 1320 a group of Scottish barons sent a letter to Pope John XXII that affirmed Scotland's independence from England.

It was a momentous event that changed Scotland's future forever. As a newly independent country, Scotland would have to tackle economic issues such as inequality and climate change. Its central bank might be limited in how much it could influence these policies without a new currency, and its public finances might face the same constraints that other countries do.

Cultural heritage, art and architecture

Scotland has a rich and diverse cultural and artistic heritage that has evolved over many centuries. Here are some key aspects of Scotland's cultural and artistic heritage:

- Music: Scotland is renowned for its traditional music, which includes the bagpipes, fiddles, and accordion. The country also has a strong history of classical music, with composers such as James MacMillan and Thea Musgrave.
- Visual arts: Scotland has a vibrant contemporary art scene, with institutions such as the National Galleries of Scotland and the Scottish National Gallery of Modern Art showcasing the work of Scottish and international artists.
- Dance: The country also has a thriving contemporary dance scene, with companies such as Scottish Ballet and the Scottish Dance Theatre.
- Theatre: Scottish playwrights such as David Greig and Liz Lochhead have achieved international acclaim.
- Film: Scotland has a rich history of filmmaking, with classic movies such as "Braveheart" and "Trainspotting" being filmed in the country. More recently, productions such as "Outlander" and "The Crown" have been filmed in Scotland.

Overall, Scotland's cultural and artistic heritage is a testament to the country's rich history and ongoing creativity. Scotland, located in the northern part of the United Kingdom, has a rich history, unique culture, and distinctive architecture. In this response, we will explore each of these aspects in more detail.

History:

Scotland's recorded history dates back to the 4th century when the Romans invaded the area. Over time, various groups, including the Picts, the Celts, and the Vikings, left their mark on the land. Scotland became a unified kingdom in the 9th century under King Kenneth MacAlpin. During the Middle Ages, Scotland experienced significant political turmoil and military conflict, including wars with England.

In the 18th century, Scotland underwent a period of rapid industrialization, with major advances in the production of textiles, iron, and coal. The country became a major player in the British Empire and made significant contributions to the fields of science, engineering, and medicine. However, Scotland also faced challenges, including poverty, political unrest, and emigration.

Culture:

Scotland has a rich cultural heritage that includes music, dance, literature, and art. Perhaps the most iconic cultural symbol of Scotland is the bagpipes, a musical instrument that has been played in Scotland for centuries. The country is also known for its traditional dances, including the Highland fling and the sword dance.

Architecture:

Scotland has a rich architectural history that spans several centuries. Some of the most iconic Scottish buildings include the Edinburgh Castle, Stirling Castle, and Eilean Donan Castle. These castles were built during the Middle Ages and served as centers of power and military defense.

Scotland is also home to many examples of Gothic architecture, including the Glasgow Cathedral and St. Giles' Cathedral in Edinburgh. The country also has many examples of Victorian architecture, including the Glasgow School of Art and the Scott Monument in Edinburgh. In addition, Scotland has a rich tradition of building stone circles and other prehistoric structures, such as the Callanish Stones on the Isle of Lewis.

In conclusion, Scotland has a rich history, unique culture, and distinctive architecture. From its turbulent past to its contributions to the arts and sciences, Scotland continues to be a fascinating and important part of the world's cultural landscape.

Chapter 2.

Itineraries

To make the most of your trip to Scotland, it's important to plan out your days and prioritize the sights and activities you want to experience. Here are some detailed itineraries for trips of different lengths to help you effectively organize your days in Scotland

3-day itinerary:

Day 1:

Explore Edinburgh: Visit the Edinburgh Castle, stroll through the Royal Mile, and admire the architecture of St Giles' Cathedral.

Walk up Arthur's Seat: Enjoy panoramic views of the city from this iconic hill.

Day 2:

Visit Stirling: Tour the Stirling Castle and the Wallace Monument.

Drive through Loch Lomond & The Trossachs National Park: Take a scenic drive through this beautiful area.

Day 3:

Take a day trip to the Isle of Skye: Visit the Fairy Pools, the Old Man of Storr, and the Quiraing.

5-day itinerary:

Day 1:

Explore Edinburgh: Visit the Edinburgh Castle, stroll through the Royal Mile, and admire the architecture of St Giles' Cathedral.

Walk up Arthur's Seat: Enjoy panoramic views of the city from this iconic hill.

Day 2:

Take a day trip to St Andrews: Visit the St Andrews Castle and Cathedral, and play a round of golf at the Old Course.

Day 3:

Visit Stirling: Tour the Stirling Castle and the Wallace Monument.

Drive through Loch Lomond & The Trossachs National Park: Take a scenic drive through this beautiful area.

Day 4:

Take a day trip to the Isle of Skye: Visit the Fairy Pools, the Old Man of Storr, and the Quiraing.

Day 5:

Explore Glasgow: Visit the Glasgow Cathedral, Kelvingrove Art Gallery and Museum, and the Glasgow Science Centre.

7-day itinerary:

Day 1:

Explore Edinburgh: Visit the Edinburgh Castle, stroll through the Royal Mile, and admire the architecture of St Giles' Cathedral.

Walk up Arthur's Seat: Enjoy panoramic views of the city from this iconic hill.

Day 2:

Take a day trip to St Andrews: Visit the St Andrews Castle and Cathedral, and play a round of golf at the Old Course.

Day 3:

Visit Stirling: Tour the Stirling Castle and the Wallace Monument.

Drive through Loch Lomond & The Trossachs National Park: Take a scenic drive through this beautiful area.

Day 4:

Take a day trip to the Isle of Skye: Visit the Fairy Pools, the Old Man of Storr, and the Quiraing.

Day 5:

Explore Glasgow: Visit the Glasgow Cathedral, Kelvingrove Art Gallery and Museum, and the Glasgow Science Centre.

Day 6:

Visit Inverness: Take a scenic drive through the Cairngorms National Park, and visit the Culloden Battlefield and Clava Cairns.

Day 7:

Take a day trip to the Isle of Mull: Visit the Duart Castle, the Isle of Iona, and the Fingal's Cave.

14-Day Itinerary

Day 1: Edinburgh

Start your Scottish adventure in the country's capital, Edinburgh. Explore the historic Old Town with its winding streets and famous Royal Mile. Visit Edinburgh Castle, perched on a hilltop overlooking the city, and the iconic St Giles' Cathedral. Wander through the charming Grassmarket area and enjoy a traditional Scottish meal in one of its many restaurants.

Day 2: St Andrews

Drive north to the charming town of St Andrews, home to the famous golf course and Scotland's oldest university. Walk along the picturesque beach and explore the ruins of St Andrews Cathedral and St Andrews Castle. In the evening, enjoy a drink at the famous Dunvegan Hotel, frequented by golfers and locals alike.

Day 3: Inverness

Travel north to Inverness, the capital of the Scottish Highlands. Take a scenic drive along the shores of Loch Ness and keep an eye out for the mythical monster. Explore the city's historic Old Town, including Inverness Castle and the impressive St Andrew's Cathedral. In the evening, sample some local whisky at a nearby distillery.

Day 4: Isle of Skye

Take a day trip to the Isle of Skye, known for its stunning landscapes and rugged coastline. Stop by the iconic Eilean Donan Castle before crossing the bridge to the island. Visit the picturesque village of Portree and explore the island's rugged landscapes, including the Old Man of Storr and the Quiraing.

Day 5: Cairngorms National Park

Drive east to Cairngorms National Park, home to some of Scotland's most stunning scenery. Take a hike through the park's dramatic landscape of mountains, forests, and lochs. In the evening, relax in one of the park's cozy lodges or enjoy a meal in one of its many local restaurants.

Day 6: Aberdeen

Visit the city of Aberdeen, known as the "Granite City" for its many gray stone buildings. Explore the city's historic Old Town, including the 13th-century St Machar's Cathedral and the famous Marischal College. Take a stroll along the beach and enjoy some fresh seafood at one of the local restaurants.

Day 7: Perthshire

Travel south to Perthshire, known as "Big Tree Country" for its beautiful forests and woodlands. Visit the famous Gleneagles Golf Course or take a hike through the picturesque countryside. In the evening, relax at a nearby spa or enjoy a meal in one of the area's many gourmet restaurants.

Day 8: Stirling

Visit the historic city of Stirling, located at the heart of Scotland. Explore Stirling Castle, one of Scotland's most important historic sites, and the nearby Wallace Monument, which commemorates the life of Scottish hero William Wallace. Take a stroll through the charming Old Town and enjoy some local cuisine.

Day 9: Glasgow

Visit Scotland's largest city, Glasgow, known for its vibrant arts and culture scene. Explore the city's many museums and galleries, including the Kelvingrove Art Gallery and Museum and the Riverside Museum. In the evening, enjoy some live music in one of the city's many music venues.

Day 10: Loch Lomond and The Trossachs National Park

Take a drive to Loch Lomond and The Trossachs National Park, known for its stunning lochs, mountains, and forests. Take a boat ride on Loch Lomond or hike through the beautiful countryside. In the evening, enjoy a meal in one of the park's many cozy pubs and restaurants.

Day 11: Oban

Visit the seaside town of Oban, known as the "Gateway to the Isles". Take a ferry to one of the nearby islands, including Mull, Iona, or Staffa.

Alternatively, explore the town's charming harbor and visit the famous Oban Distillery, which produces some of Scotland's best-known whisky.

Day 12: Fort William

Visit the town of Fort William, located at the foot of Ben Nevis, Scotland's highest mountain. Take a scenic drive along the famous Road to the Isles and visit the stunning

Glenfinnan Viaduct, famous for its appearance in the Harry Potter movies. In the evening, relax at a nearby spa or enjoy some local cuisine.

Day 13: Perth

Visit the city of Perth, located on the banks of the River Tay. Explore the historic city center, including the beautiful St John's Kirk and the Perth Museum and Art Gallery. Take a stroll along the river and enjoy some local cuisine in one of the city's many restaurants.

Day 14: Fife

Explore the beautiful region of Fife, located just north of Edinburgh. Visit the picturesque fishing villages of

Anstruther and Crail and enjoy some fresh seafood. Take a walk along the beautiful beach at St Andrews or visit the historic town of Dunfermline, once the royal capital of Scotland.

This 14-day itinerary offers a varied and exciting tour of Scotland, with something for everyone, from the historic cities of Edinburgh and Stirling to the rugged wilderness of the Scottish Highlands and the beautiful coastlines of Fife and Oban.

These itineraries can be adjusted to suit your interests and preferences, but they provide a good starting point for planning your trip to Scotland.

Map of Glasgow

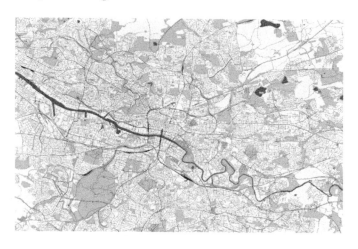

Map of Edimburgh

Map of Aberdeen

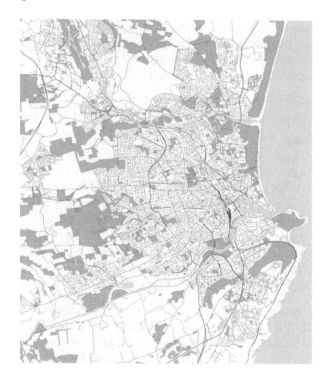

Tips on when it is best to go sightseeing

The best time to go sightseeing is when there aren't too many people around. This is because the crowds can become a nuisance and you don't want to spend your vacation stuck in line for hours just to get in!

To minimize these hassles, book your tickets online or in advance. Some attractions even offer skip-the-line tickets.

Spring

Spring (March-May) and Autumn (September-November): These seasons offer beautiful scenery with colorful blooms in spring and autumnal foliage in the fall. The weather can be unpredictable, but it's generally milder than winter, making it a great time to explore the country's castles, museums, and galleries. It's also a good time to visit the Highlands and islands when the crowds are fewer, and the accommodation prices are lower.

Spring is a great time to travel for many reasons. It's an ideal time to see blossoming flowers and trees, and it's a good chance to visit destinations that aren't as crowded as in other seasons. It's also a good time to save money on flights and accommodation, so it can be the perfect time to plan your next adventure!

Another thing to consider is the weather. You'll want to check the local climate and pack a few layers of clothing. For example, if you're visiting an area with a cold, rainy climate, then it's best to bring a light jacket and an umbrella just in case.

Summer

Summer (June-August): This is the peak tourist season in Scotland, with long daylight hours and mild weather. It's the best time to go sightseeing if you want to explore the country's outdoors and enjoy outdoor activities such as hiking, cycling, and wildlife watching. It's also the time when many festivals take place, such as the Edinburgh Festival Fringe, the Royal Highland Show, and the Scottish Traditional Boat Festival.

Winter

Winter is a wonderful time to visit many destinations in the world, as it offers great weather, low season rates and a chance to experience some of the best holiday attractions in the country.

Winter (December-February): Winter is the least popular time to visit Scotland due to its cold weather and shorter daylight hours. It's also a great time to visit Scotland's cities and enjoy the festive season, including Hogmanay, the Scottish New Year celebration, and Burns Night, which honors the famous poet Robert Burns.

It's essential to check the weather forecast and plan your itinerary accordingly to make the most of your trip.

Safety precautions while in Scotland

Safety is always a concern when traveling to a new country, but Scotland is one of the safest places in Europe. The crime rate is very low, especially in big cities like Edinburgh and Glasgow, and there are many precautions you can take to ensure your safety while touring Scotland.

1. Keep your belongings safe

There's no denying that traveling to Scotland can be stressful if your important belongings are lost or stolen. That's why it's always a good idea to take safety precautions while you're out and about.

If you're looking for ways to keep your things safe, one of the most effective strategies is to divide them between multiple bags and pockets. You can do this with your wallet, travel documents and even your camera! It's also a good idea to carry an extra phone charger so you can charge your devices while you're out and about.

You can also add a pocket pouch to your travel bag so that you can keep your passport, cash and credit cards in there. This will make it easier for you to access your items without having to open up your bag every time.

As for what to wear while visiting Scotland, it's a good idea to invest in some quality clothing. This can include a woollen jacket, hat or scarf. These will keep you warm, dry and lightweight.

2. Don't wander aimlessly

When you are in Scotland, it is important to keep safety precautions in mind.

This is especially true if you are planning to go hiking, as it can be dangerous for travelers who are not familiar with the terrain.

If you are a traveler who enjoys the outdoors, you should definitely consider visiting Scotland.

3. Don't go hiking on your own

Hiking can be a great way to see Scotland's breathtaking scenery, but it's important to know your limits. Make sure you're physically fit and can handle a long-distance hike, and always be prepared for weather changes. It's not for the faint of heart, but it's a must-do for any walker who wants to connect with nature.

4. Don't stand too close to the water

If you plan on visiting the coast while in Scotland, it is important to avoid standing too close to the water. The waves in the North Atlantic can be big and unexpected, so it is best to stay in a safe area where you can leave if a large swell comes up.

In addition to being a great place for hiking and exploring, Scotland is also known for its wild beaches. This makes it a popular destination for travelers who want to spend time in the outdoors without having to worry about safety.

Another great way to enjoy the outdoors in Scotland is to go on a boat tour. Whether it is on Loch Ness, one of the most famous lochs in Scotland, or on the Isle of Skye, this is a great way to see some of the most beautiful scenery in the country.

When traveling in the Highlands, be careful on single-track roads. These roads are often narrow and twisted. It is essential to understand the local driving laws and standards so you don't end up in an accident.

5. Don't drink alcohol

It can impair your judgment, coordination, and reaction time, which increases your risk of accidents and injuries.

Many people don't think about this, but there are a lot of places in Scotland that won't allow you to drink. This includes bars, restaurants, and clubs. If you're not sure whether you can drink in a particular location, check with the local government first.

6. Don't trespass

If you're planning on going on a vacation to Scotland, you'll want to make sure that you follow all safety precautions while in the country. One of these precautions involves not trespassing on other people's property.

In some cases, trespassing may be considered a criminal offence, and the person who is trespassing can face charges. This usually happens when someone enters private property or a place where they are not allowed to be, such as a store or a city park.

A trespasser is usually charged with the third degree of trespassing, which carries a maximum sentence of six months in jail. The Scottish Outdoor Access Code provides guidance to both land owners and members of the public regarding how they should behave when accessing land. This includes respecting other people's privacy and peace of mind, as well as taking care to not harm the environment.

7. Don't leave your passport in your hotel room

If you're travelling to Scotland with a passport from another country, it's important that you check whether you need a visa before you leave.

If you plan on visiting Scotland for business or study purposes, you should apply for a visa before you travel to ensure your entry is granted. This can be done online or in person at the embassy.

To avoid being robbed, keep your passport in your hotel room safe and carry a photocopy of it with you when you leave. Also, don't leave any large amounts of cash in your luggage when you're not in the hotel.

What to avoid

From hiking the Highlands to enjoying a deep-fried chocolate bar, there are so many things you can do while visiting this beautiful place!

1. Not planning ahead

Planning ahead means booking accommodation in advance and scouting out the best deals for your trip. This will also give you a better chance of getting the best deals on attractions and activities during your visit.

Another great tip is to check out online timetables for all of the services that you will be using during your stay in Scotland. This will help you to avoid long journeys or being stuck on the road for hours on end.

Finally, it is important to remember that Scotland is a country full of unique experiences and sights. This makes it a very special place to visit.

Whether you are looking to visit the highlands or explore Edinburgh, Scotland has something for everyone. Whether you are into hiking, exploring historical sites, or even trying your hand at highland dancing or haggis hurling, there is something for everyone in Scotland.

2. Not bringing the right gear

If you're planning on traveling in Scotland, it's important to bring the right gear. This will ensure that you have everything you need while staying comfortable and warm. You'll also save money on accommodation and gas.

For example, if you're going to be camping or doing long hikes, it's best to pack a tent and sleeping bag instead of buying these items on your trip. This will not only save you money, but it will also help the planet as well.

Another key piece of equipment to bring on your Scotland trip is a backpack. This will make carrying all of your essentials so much easier! You'll be able to carry water bottles, snacks, a camera, and more in one handy bag.

A hat and scarf are also essential to travel with in Scotland as they will protect you from windy weather. They are also a great way to add a touch of style to your outfit.

You should also take a lightweight water bottle, especially if you're doing a lot of hiking or walking. A collapsible water bottle is a good choice because it's light and folds up easily when you're not using it.

3. Not packing for the weather

Scotland is a stunning land that's full of wonder and beauty at every turn. Its lush landscapes, towering mountains, and wild white beaches make it a must-visit destination for anyone traveling to the United Kingdom.

But the weather in Scotland can change quickly and often, making it crucial to pack for the weather when traveling. This is especially important if you plan to explore the outdoors, where rain and wind can bring a chill to your vacation.

It's also worth adding a waterproof rain jacket to your Scotland packing list, as this is one piece of gear that you won't want to miss out on! Besides being extremely handy in the rain, this jacket will help keep you warm and cozy while fighting off the chills, too.

If you're planning to spend a lot of time outdoors, be sure to pack a hat and gloves, too. The cold can be brutal in Scotland, and you'll want to protect your head from the elements as much as possible.

Likewise, be sure to bring some insect repellant along with you. There are a number of different bugs that are common throughout Scotland, and you'll likely be exposed to them while you're on your vacation.

Whether you're heading to Scotland for a romantic getaway or an adventure of a lifetime, making sure to pack the right items will help ensure your trip is stress-free and memorable!

4. Not looking for the best deals

There are many ways to save money while traveling in Scotland, from using public transport instead of renting a car or taking taxis to finding budget-friendly hotel rooms. These tips can help you avoid unnecessary expenses and make the most of your time in this beautiful country.

Another way to save on your hotel stay is to book in advance. Ideally, you should book at least 67 days before your trip begins to ensure you get the best deal on your hotel room.

For dining out, it is important to look for lunch deals as this can be a lot cheaper than dinner. A two- or three-course meal at a restaurant can cost up to PS20-25 during lunchtime, which is a significant savings over dinner.

It is also a good idea to carry a travel card, debit or credit card with you so that you can pay for hotel stays, food and gas without incurring foreign transaction fees. The Capital One VentureOne Rewards Credit Card is a great option that doesn't charge these fees when you swipe it.

5. Not taking advantage of travel passes

If you want to save time and money while traveling in Scotland, you need to be on the lookout for travel passes.

These are available to cover train, bus and ferry routes and usually include several days worth of travel.

You can get these passes at most railway stations in Scotland and can be very useful for covering multiple cities if you're planning to visit a number of places. You can also purchase these passes in advance to save yourself the hassle of buying tickets at each station when you arrive.

In addition to using a travel pass, you should also look out for off-peak fares on ScotRail trains. These fares are less expensive during the week and can be found by looking on their website.

Another way to save on transport in Scotland is by taking buses rather than trains. You can often find a Megabus ticket for a fraction of the price of a train fare and you can often get these fares by booking them ahead of time.

6. Not joining a guided tour

Scotland is a beautiful country and there is so much to see. Joining a guided tour is a great way to see Scotland at its best, as they are experts in their area and can share with you all of the top Scottish sights.

The beauty of a guided tour is that you will have your own local guide who will know all of the hidden gems and tell you all about the stories behind the places you visit. They will also be able to answer any questions you may have about the history, language and customs of Scotland.

Another great thing about guided tours is that they are usually very cost-effective. They are a lot cheaper than hiring your own car and they will often include all of the insurance, fuel and parking costs for you.

As well as saving you money on travel, taking a coach tour will allow you to enjoy the stunning scenery throughout your journey. You will be able to drive up and down the mountains and see the beautiful sea views as you go along.

Lastly, guided tours are an excellent way to save money on food. You will be able to buy a lot of meals from budget supermarkets and you can even get some nice lunch specials in some restaurants.

Chapter 3.

Scotland's top attractions

A mighty fortress and a world-famous tourist attraction, Edinburgh Castle dominates the Scottish skyline. It has a long history, with countless sieges and battles over the years.

Visitors can explore the various highlights of this mighty fortress on a guided tour. Besides learning about its history, travelers will get to experience stunning panoramic views of the city from this vantage point.

1. St. Margaret's Chapel

St. Margaret's Chapel is a hidden gem located in Edinburgh, Scotland. The chapel is located within the grounds of Edinburgh Castle and is named after St. Margaret, who was the queen of Scotland in the 11th century. It was originally used as a private chapel for the royal family, and it is said that St. Margaret herself used to pray in the chapel.

Despite its age, the chapel has been well-preserved over the years. It features beautiful stained-glass windows, stone carvings, and a vaulted ceiling. The chapel also contains an altar and a small altar room, which were added in the 1920s. Its peaceful atmosphere and stunning design make it a hidden gem that is definitely worth a visit.

2. The Royal Palace

The palace was built in the 16th century by King James IV of Scotland, who used it as a hunting lodge. It was later expanded by King James V and became a favorite residence of the Stuart monarchs. Mary, Queen of Scots, was known to have stayed at the palace on several occasions, and it was also a favorite of King Charles I.

The palace is home to an impressive collection of artwork, tapestries, and furniture, which provide a glimpse into the life and times of the Scottish monarchs who lived there.

One of the highlights of the palace is its beautiful gardens, which feature a variety of plants and flowers, as well as several ornamental ponds and fountains.

3. Edinburgh Castle

The castle is perched on top of a hill in the heart of the city and offers stunning views of the surrounding area. The castle dates back to the 12th century and has been the site of numerous battles and historical events over the years. Today, it is one of the most popular tourist attractions in Scotland, with millions of visitors flocking to see its historic architecture, museums, and exhibits.

One of the highlights of the castle is the Royal Palace, which features beautiful rooms and exhibits that showcase the lives of the Scottish monarchs who lived there. Visitors can also explore the Great Hall, which dates back to the 16th century and is known for its stunning architecture and historic artifacts.

The castle also features several museums and exhibits, including the National War Museum of Scotland, which showcases the country's military history, and the Scottish National War Memorial, which honors those who have died in conflict.

In addition to its historical and cultural significance, Edinburgh Castle also offers stunning views of the city and the surrounding area. Visitors can take a guided tour of the castle and learn about its history and significance, or simply wander around and take in the sights and sounds of this iconic landmark.

4. The One O'Clock Gun

A gleaming WWII 25-pounder fires an ear-splitting time signal at 1pm every day (except on Sunday, Christmas Day and Good Friday). The tradition began in 1861 when a gun was fired from Edinburgh Castle to provide ships sailing in the Firth of Forth with an audible signal for setting their chronometers.

The One O'Clock Gun is a unique feature of the Castle and is a must-see for visitors who are interested in Scotland's military history. It is also a great spot to take in the views of the New Town below.

The One O'Clock Gun is located on Mills Mount Battery, which sits to the north of the castle. From this vantage point, you can see the battlements and the Royal Mile.

5. The Scottish Crown Jewels

The Scottish Crown Jewels (also known as the Honours of Scotland) are a jewel encrusted crown, elaborate sword and sceptre that were used for coronation ceremonies throughout Scotland's history. Today, they're on display at Edinburgh Castle.

In the 15th century, monarchs in Scotland wore these crowning symbols to represent their new status as ruler. The crown, sword and sceptre were originally made for

King James V of Scotland and are the oldest surviving Crown Jewels in Britain.

They've been hidden multiple times to prevent them from being stolen or destroyed. But now they're back on display at Edinburgh Castle, where they remain a symbol of Scotland's royal heritage and cultural significance.

There are plenty of other things to see and do inside the castle too. But we recommend you start your tour with the Crown Jewels, then move on to other areas at your leisure. To avoid long lines, purchase tickets online before you arrive in Edinburgh.

6.The Great Hall

Edinburgh Castle is one of the most iconic sights in Europe. Atop a volcanic rock, it dominates the city skyline and is a symbol of Scotland's history.

It's a must see on any trip to the city and you won't regret visiting. You'll get to see the Scottish crown jewels, enjoy panoramic views of Edinburgh and watch the famous time signal, the One O'Clock Gun.

You can also visit the cavernous stone vaults beneath the Great Hall that once held prisoners of war. These have been restored to their former state and you'll be able to see original graffiti that was carved by prisoners.

The Great Hall has a long history and is filled with exciting stories. It's where Mary Queen of Scots sat down to enjoy a banquet and where the famous One O'Clock Gun was fired.

7. The National War Museum

The National War Museum, located inside Edinburgh Castle, is a fascinating place to learn about the history of Scotland at war. It's run by National Museums Scotland and covers 400 years of Scottish involvement in battle, from the 17th century all the way up to modern military service.

Visitors can explore the museum's collection of weapons, uniforms, and military equipment. They'll also see a selection of paintings of battlefields, as well as personal treasures from soldiers who've gone to foreign campaigns.

The National War Museum is one of the most popular paid-for attractions in Edinburgh. It's housed within three ranges of buildings that were built around Hospital Square in the 1700s by William Skinner as storehouses for ordnance.

8. The Castle's Battlements

If you want to get a feel for how life would have been in a castle, it's a good idea to visit one of Scotland's mighty ruins. Dunnottar is one of the most iconic and photogenic, but it's not the only castle to take pride of place on a rocky hill.

Eilean Donan is another ruined castle that's well known for its beauty and stunning location. This tidal island is located at the confluence of Loch Long and Loch Duich, and has been a fortress since the 13th century.

Linlithgow Palace is a historic building that has seen a number of famous monarchs come and go. Both Mary Queen of Scots and James V were born here, so it's a must-visit on any trip to Scotland.

At the center of a bloody feud between the Forbes and Gordon clans, Congarff Castle was torched in 1571. It was later rebuilt and used as a garrison by government forces following the Battle of Culloden in 1746.

9. The Royal Mile

It is a maze of tall, medieval buildings peppered with souvenir shops, lively drinking and dining spots and historical landmarks like the Scottish Parliament and St Giles' Cathedral.

The Royal Mile is also home to a number of superb attractions including the Real Mary King's Close, the Scottish Storytelling Centre, and many museums. The People's Story Museum is particularly interesting, as it focuses on the life of Scotland's working class from the 18th century through to the 20th.

The Royal Mile is also home to some of the city's best restaurants and pubs, so you can indulge in some good food while enjoying the stunning views over Arthur's Seat. You can even visit the world-famous Camera Obscura, a five-floor optical illusion museum that is a must-see for anyone visiting Edinburgh.

The hidden gems of Scotland

There are countless classic views and unique sights to be seen in Scotland, but there are also lots of places that are more hidden and out of the way.

These secret spots offer that special sense of adventure that we all crave when visiting Scotland. Let's explore some of these hidden gems!

Corrimony Nature Reserve

Corrimony Nature Reserve is a great place to get back to nature and relax in the stunning moorland scenery of Glen Urquhart, near Loch Ness. The 1530 hectares of open moorland and sections of Caledonian forest are managed by the RSPB, which means that you'll have the chance to see some of Scotland's most iconic wildlife. During springtime, you can watch lekking black grouse display their courtship skills, while spotted flycatchers, crested tits and wood warblers will also be found here.

If you're an animal lover, this reserve is a paradise for roe deer, red and pine martens, wild goat, otters and hares. Dogs are welcome, but please be aware of your pet's behaviour and don't let them off the lead during breeding season as they can cause damage to nesting birds.

This hidden gem is home to a number of historical sites and has some truly beautiful views. You can walk amongst a circle of standing stones and discover the

Corrimony chambered cairn, which dates back 4,000 years, or visit Mony's Stone, an ancient passage grave built by the neolithic people who lived in the area.

The chambered cairn is one of the most amazing examples of a Clava type cairn, and has been preserved for over 4,000 years. It is thought that the cairn was used as a burial site, and the builders were skilled in working stone. The cairn is surrounded by 11 stones and has prehistoric rock art on the capstone.

There is no charge for visiting Corrimony, but a donation is appreciated to help keep the site in good condition. In addition to the cairn, you can find a stone circle, a burial site and a small burial ground.

Another fascinating part of this reserve is the waterfall, which flows from a small tributary. It is an impressive sight that stretches for nearly 200 feet.

Corrimony Nature Reserve is a real hidden gem and is perfect for birders and anyone who enjoys the outdoors. With a range of native trees, wetlands, and mountain habitats, this RSPB reserve is the perfect spot to watch Scottish crossbills, black grouse and other iconic species.

Loch Rannoch

The mystical and majestic Loch Rannoch is one of the most beautiful spots in Scotland. Located near the heart of the country, it appeals to both Scots and tourists from across the world.

For those who love hiking, a visit to the Rannoch area will be an unforgettable experience. The surrounding countryside is dotted with a number of Munroes, and walking and climbing trails are readily available. The conical mountain, dubbed Schiehallion, is the main attraction in the area, although easier hillwalking and nature trails also await.

If you're interested in learning about the history of this area, a stroll along the Clan Trail will provide an interesting insight into the region's past. A series of story boards are scattered around the loch shore and tell fascinating stories about the various clans that have occupied the region in the past.

Another fascinating place to explore is the hamlet of Kinloch Rannoch, which was created in the post-1745 period. He was determined to improve the lot of the inhabitants, bringing in more schools, building bridges and erecting church buildings. He also provided food and introduced new farming methods.

Eventually, the community of Rannoch became civilized and no more thefts or robberies were heard from the village residents. In 1761, the General Assembly of the Church of Scotland recognized that this small settlement was now becoming a model for other Highland communities.

A visit to Loch Rannoch is a must for anyone who loves the outdoors and wants to see some of the most stunning natural beauty in the world. You'll find plenty to do here, from swimming in the mystical waters of Loch Rannoch to exploring the ancient forests and wild moorland in the surrounding area.

Falls of Truim

If you're looking for a beautiful waterfall in the Cairngorms, then Falls of Truim is well worth the effort. Just a short walk from the main road, you can see this set of cascades in a quiet gorge. The falls aren't a single drop, but rather a series of rapids, with countless potholes and pools created by centuries of river erosion.

After leaving the car park, follow the road on foot and you'll soon come across an old military bridge that straddles the river. From here, you can take a few steps down to the river and see the falls up close. You can also enjoy the views of Slioch and Loch Maree from here.

While you're in this part of Scotland, make sure to try out the distillery at Dalwhinnie. This distillery is the highest in the country, and produces a renowned whisky that is loved by all. You can visit the distillery for PS12 (or PS20 if you wish to get a bottle of your own).

Another great place to see in this region is Glen Feshie, which has inspired many artists throughout the ages. This glen is famous for its enchanting Scots pine woods and the River Feshie that flows through it.

To get to Glen Feshie, head east from Aviemore on the A9 and then turn right at the sign for Glen Feshie. If you're looking to explore further in the area, there are plenty of hidden gems waiting for you. The Four Border Abbeys are a popular day trip from Edinburgh or Glasgow, and they're filled with history.

You can also take a drive to Bealach na Ba, one of the most beautiful passes in Scotland. This is an epic road that connects the west coast with the Highlands and offers stunning views of the mountains.

Fairy Glen

If you're visiting Skye, you have to make time for the iconic Fairy Glen, an enchanting landscape that looks like something out of a fantasy film. The glen, which forms part of Glen Uig on the Trotternish Peninsula, is a short walk from the village of Uig and offers a stunning backdrop for exploring with family or friends.

The glen is an off-the-beaten-path gem, set apart from the surrounding farmland by a collection of cone-shaped hills, strangely shaped boulders, ponds, and other natural rock formations. The glen has been named as one of the

Isle of Skye's hidden gems, and it is certainly worth a visit if you want to get away from the crowds and see some of the island's most scenic landscapes.

A particularly striking feature of the Fairy Glen is Castle Ewan, a towering rock formation that looks like an ancient castle clinging to a tiny lochan in the middle of the glen. This is actually a natural outcrop of basalt (volcanic) rock that's been built upon by the elements over thousands of years.

You can visit the Fairy Glen on foot from the village of Uig, or you can hire a car to drive there and park it in the dedicated car park that's a few hundred metres from the heart of the glen. The most popular route is to walk from the car park, along a path that passes Castle Ewan and leads to a small natural chamber in the cliff.

There are also several good paths that wind around the glen, but be aware that it can be muddy and slippery in the winter months (November-March). It's also a prime location for packs of midges, so be sure to carry some midge deterrent if you plan to visit during this period.

The best time to explore the Fairy Glen is during the summer months, when it's at its most magical and when there are fewer people. Getting there early is recommended, as parking spots can get quite full during peak times and the glen can be very busy.

Chapter 4.

Local Culture in Scotland

Scottish culture is a vibrant, living thing that continues to evolve. It's also a place where history is still woven into the landscape and old traditions continue to guide modern life.

1. The People

Scotland is a fascinating country with a rich history and a diverse population. Whether you are here to visit or have made the move from another country, there is always something new and interesting to learn about our nation.

In the Middle Ages, many of Scotland's people emigrated from the area to other parts of Europe and beyond. This was a great boost to the economy and social life of Scotland.

However, this also had a significant impact on the culture of Scotland, as people became more and more influenced by their new home countries. For instance, the Scottish language merged with English to form a distinctive Scots language, and many of Scotland's national songs and dances incorporated elements of other languages such as Irish, Celtic and Germanic.

2. The Land

Scotland, the northern half of Great Britain, is a country that's largely different to England. The land is mountainous, but there are also long deep valleys, lochs and ribbon lakes that attract visitors from all over the world.

A long geological story has shaped the land and this is at the heart of what makes it special. It's part of a story that spans more than three billion years, as the earth has moved around the planet.

Geodiversity is a key feature of Scotland's landscape, with rock and soil properties influencing both land use and transport routes. Edinburgh's underlying sedimentary rocks, for example, have fundamentally shaped its physical appearance.

As with any countryside, Scotland has its own unique traditions that are deeply bound up in its physical and cultural landscape. One such tradition is the ghillie, who has been part of Scottish life since the 16th century.

The ghillies' expertise, and their constant presence on the ground, has kept them firmly within Scotland's rural identity. This is one of the reasons it's so rare to find a ghillie elsewhere in the world.

3. The Food

The food of Scotland is incredibly rich and has a lot to offer. It is a combination of traditional Scottish dishes as well as some modern Scottish cuisines.

The Scottish food focuses on simple ingredients and a high reliance on local produce such as fish, seafood, dairy products, vegetables and fruits. It is also free of additives that you may find in other types of cuisines.

One of the main traditional foods of Scotland is porridge which was a staple in the ancient times of Scotland. It is made with oats, water and salt.

Another famous dish of Scotland is shortbread which has been a favourite throughout the world for centuries. It is a sweet and delicious treat with many different flavours.

If you are planning a trip to Scotland then be sure to include traditional Scottish meals in your itinerary as well as some of the most popular drinks that are associated with the country such as Irn-Bru which is a carbonated drink made from fruit. You can also check out some of the many festivals that are held across Scotland to get a deeper insight into the culture and traditions of the country!

4. The Music

Traditional music is a hugely important part of Scottish culture. It takes many forms and has been around for thousands of years, so if you want to discover more about the genre you can find plenty of traditional music festivals throughout the country.

The main styles include Gaelic songs, ballads and laments, and Scots dance music such as jigs, reels and strathspeys. The latter is usually performed by a dance band and typically includes fiddle (violin), accordion, bagpipe and percussion.

Another important part of Scottish music is the bagpipe, a distinctively highland instrument that has been in use for centuries. Its origin is unclear, but it was probably brought to Scotland from Ireland or far beyond.

The instrument is commonly associated with Scottish folk music, though it has also been embraced by popular country dance bands. It has long been derided as kitsch, but performers such as Phil Cunningham (of Silly Wizard) have helped dispel this perception.

5. The Arts

The arts are a hugely important part of the fabric of society, providing social connections and building a sense of identity. In Scotland, a diverse range of different forms of culture exist and people are proud to live in places where their heritage is celebrated.

There are many ways to engage in and experience Scottish culture and there are a number of important museums, galleries and performance spaces across the country where access is free. Glasgow-based Kelvingrove Art Gallery and Museum is a great place to start.

Aberdeen Art Gallery is also a cultural hotspot. Its collection is recognised as a Collection of National Significance and it hosts a range of interesting exhibitions each year.

The traditional arts have a big impact on the fabric of Scottish culture and the country has many organisations that work to preserve and promote these traditions.

6. The Sport

As you would expect, sport is a hugely significant part of local culture in Scotland. Whether it be football, rugby or golf, people in Scotland take sports very seriously and have an inherited 'team' that they pass down to their children like a cherished tradition.

In fact, a significant proportion of the population can be spotted at a sporting event during any given day in Scotland. The number of people attending football matches alone has been calculated to be one in 20 per capita, a stat that is unrivalled by any other nation.

The Highland Games have also been a significant part of Scottish cultural life for many centuries. These events featured a wide range of sporting events and traditional aspects of Scottish culture such as the bagpipes.

During the early modern period, these events became more organised and standardised. The Highland Games today are a celebration of Scottish culture and offer visitors an exciting opportunity to witness an important aspect of the local community. They are often run by a non-profit organisation and are a great example of how tourism can help to bring communities together.

7. The Beliefs

There are many beliefs that influence the way we live in Scotland. While Christianity has always been the dominant religion in Scotland, other faiths such as Judaism, Buddhism and Hinduism also have a strong presence in Scotland.

Scottish culture has developed over a thousand years and the traditions are still very much alive today. These traditions are not something that are kept in a museum and they are constantly evolving.

Historically, Scotland was part of a family of polytheistic faiths that emphasized natural harmony and worshiped the gods of the earth. During the 6th century, the region converted to Christianity through the work of St. Columba, who travelled to the island of Iona and established a school that was to draw monks from England, Ireland, and Europe.

Although the majority of Scots are non-religious, religious tensions have occasionally risen to the surface. This can be a result of different opinions about life, public policy or the consequences of global conflicts. In these circumstances it is important that dialogue is fostered in a sincere and honest manner, to ensure that all can live peacefully in Scotland.

Chatting with experts on the Speyside Whisky Trail

The Speyside region is home to half of all whisky distilleries in Scotland. It also hosts the world's only whisky trail that takes visitors to seven world-famous distilleries.

The best way to enjoy the spirit is to travel with a bespoke guide who can help you experience the most of what this amazing area has to offer. Whether you want to visit the Spirit of Speyside Festival or spend some time exploring the many stunning distilleries, a personal escort can make your trip memorable and completely unique.

Benromach

The Speyside Whisky Trail is a fantastic place to visit if you're keen on sampling some of the finest single malts in Scotland. You'll find a range of distilleries on this route, all with their own unique charms and character.

A classic Speyside whisky, Benromach is made using traditional methods and has a subtle smoky character that's matured in first-fill casks. This single malt is a favourite amongst whisky enthusiasts, winning gold at the 2014 World Whisky Awards.

To get to Benromach, head north from Forres on the A96 and take Waterford Road. The distillery is on your left as you turn round towards the railway line.

There's a large visitor centre here where you can watch the distilling process and learn more about the history of the site. You can also book a tour of the distillery or visit the shop.

The Speyside Cooperage is a great stop off along the trail. You can see the casks that whisky is bottled in being made and also learn about the ancient art of coopering. This is a fascinating activity that you should definitely add to your trip.

Cardhu

If you're looking for an adventure in your whisky tasting journey, then a Speyside Whisky Trail tour is a great option. From Buckie to Aviemore, this secluded route takes you through rolling hills, forests and coastlines. However, it is not recommended for those who are not in good physical shape.

Cardhu is one of the distilleries that you can visit on the Speyside Whisky Trail, and is also known as the spiritual home of Johnnie Walker. Its mellow character is a reflection of its time-consuming distillation process.

It was founded in 1824 by a whisky smuggler named John Cumming, and today it is owned by Diageo. Its production is used in many blends, including Johnnie Walker Black Label, but it still maintains its single malt status.

Aside from being a great introduction to the Speyside region of Scotland, a visit to Cardhu is a unique experience in itself. There are several options to choose from, including a Collection Tour where you will taste five different Cardhu Single Malt Whiskies.

The distillery also hosts a number of events and festivals, and you can take part in them. They are a fantastic way to meet other whisky lovers and make new friends.

Glenfiddich

As the world's leading single malt whisky distiller, Glenfiddich sells more than 1.22 million 9-liter cases annually. It's located in Dufftown, Scotland and is owned by William Grant & Sons, who also own Balvenie Distillery.

Its stag icon — a stag spotted in the valley from which it takes its name — represents its ethos of looking to the future and pushing forward, according to brand communications manager Giardina. It was originally based on a painting by Sir Edwin Landseer, but has evolved into a symbol that speaks to the brand's heritage of being inspired by nature and its place in Scottish culture.

Founded in 1886, it's one of the most popular brands in the industry, and is considered an iconic part of the Speyside Whisky Trail. Its bottlings have won more awards since 2000 than any other single malt Scotch.

The company's bestselling expression is the 12-year-old, which offers an excellent value for money and wide appeal. Its sweet apple flavor dominates the nose and is complemented by light honey and vanilla. It's not a complex whisky, but it is satisfying and enjoyable.

The distillery's cask selection is made in-house, with the most important component being Robbie Dhu spring water. It's added to the selected distillate in a spirit safe to 63% alcohol before it is placed into oak casks from around the world and left to mature. This process can take up to 30 years.

Glenlivet

Located in the Speyside whisky region, Glenlivet is a popular distillery that sells around six million bottles of single malt scotch annually. Founded in 1823, the distillery is a popular choice for travelers looking to learn about Scotland's most famous single malt whisky and the craft behind its production.

Visitors to the distillery can take a tour of the facility and experience its production process firsthand. They'll walk through a barley-lined walkway, and learn about the people that work here from the farmers who grow the barley to the warehouse workers to the master distiller.

In addition to a traditional tour, Glenlivet offers a Legacy Tasting Experience where visitors can sample rare drams, learn about the history of the distillery and take home a gift. You can also stop by the cooperage and witness the ancient art of making a barrel from start to finish.

The tasting room at the distillery is a cosy space that reflects the distillery's location and uses natural materials to create a warm atmosphere. It includes a bar, lounge area, shop with fill your own bottle stations and an archive area that highlights the brand's history.

Glenlivet has a wide range of whiskeys that have been aged in various types of casks, including sherry, port, and cognac barrels. These single cask offerings can be a great way to try a different flavor profile of their standard expressions, and you may just discover one that's just right for you.

Strathisla

The Speyside Whisky Trail is a long-distance hiking route that takes you through some of Scotland's most beautiful landscapes. It's a perfect fit for those who enjoy hiking, but are also a fan of whisky.

The trail is a 72-mile loop around the Speyside region, passing through railway lines and rolling hills that make it a challenging route for anyone with a moderate level of fitness. There are shorter options for those who prefer a less strenuous journey.

Strathisla is one of the oldest distilleries in the Speyside region. It's located in Keith, not far from some of the most spectacular views you can find in Scotland.

It's owned by the luxury brand Chivas Brothers and is a key part of their Chivas Regal blend. They produce four stills that burn approximately million liters of whiskey every year.

At the distillery you can chat with experts on the Speyside Whisky Trail and learn about the production of single malt whiskey. They'll share their knowledge and give you a taste of some of the finest whiskies they have to offer.

They'll talk about how whiskies are blended and the rare skills needed to create prestigious whiskies. They'll also help you to discover the subtleties of each whisky as you 'nose' them.

Whether you're an experienced whisky lover or a first-timer, your visit to Strathisla will be a truly memorable experience.

Dallas Dhu

The Speyside Whisky Trail is a fantastic way to immerse yourself in the history of this beautiful area. It also gives you the chance to sample world-famous single malt Scotch whisky and enjoy a range of traditional activities.

One of the more unusual stops on this route is Dallas Dhu, a former distillery that has a fascinating chequered history. It was conceived by local entrepreneur Alexander Edward in 1898 and eventually closed for production in 1983.

During the mid-19th century, many whisky distilleries were built with a distinctive 'pointy roof' design - similar to the ones used at ancient Buddhist temples. The roofs were first used at the Dailuaine distillery in 1889 and they were later installed at dozens of other Scottish whisky distilleries.

While the roof may seem out of place in Scotland, it has a long and interesting history here. The origins of the pointy roof are Scottish, and the design was originally created by Charles Doig and his two sons who worked on the design of over a hundred distilleries across both Ireland and Scotland.

The distillery has a long two-story malt barn where until 1968 all of the malt for the distillery was produced. They stopped using their own malt in 1968 and instead began sourcing their malt from the industrial SMD Maltings plant located in nearby Burghead.

On your tour you can chat with the experts who will explain how the whisky is made at Dallas Dhu, and give you a taste of some of the different whiskies produced here. They'll tell you about the distillery's unique features and provide a great insight into its history.

Cheering on the locals at a Highland Games event

The Highland Games are one of Scotland's oldest traditions. They feature tartan kilts, bagpipes, whisky and much joviality.

They're also a great way to celebrate local culture and heritage. Attendees cheer on athletes and dancers while learning about their country's history.

Cheer on the athletes.

These events were originally impromptu sports at clan gatherings, but have since expanded into international athletic meets. Today, they are held in more than 180 countries worldwide.

Traditionally, competitors at Highland Games wear kilts and carry bagpipes. The games were first held in Scotland, but they are now found in many places around the world, including the United States and Canada.

Another event that is fun to watch is the stone put, where competitors try to throw a heavy stone as far as possible.

The stone is sourced from a local river and usually weighs around 20lb.

It is important to note that the heavy events at Highland Games are very tough and require a lot of strength. The ideal athlete will have strong legs to help them lift the weights, as well as good core and upper body strength.

Some of the most popular heavy events at Highland Games are the caber toss, the hammer throw and the weight over bar. The caber toss is an exclusively Highland event that involves throwing a large tapered pole called a "caber." This is made from larch wood and can weigh up to 79 pounds (31 kg).

Other traditional heavy events at the games are the hammer throw, weight over bar, the stone carry and the Scottish hammer, where competitors carry a 22-pound weight on their back while standing.

The heavy events at the Phoenix Scottish Games were introduced in 1982. They were created to preserve Scottish highland athletics, which had been largely lost in the years after WWII. They are a great way to get people involved in the sport and give them an opportunity to compete against other athletes.

Cheer on the dancers.

A Highland Games event is a great way to enjoy Scottish culture and tradition. Whether you want to watch the heavy events, dance with the locals or shop for souvenirs, it's a chance to experience something truly unique.

The locals at these events are often dressed in traditional kilts and will be performing dances to the music of bagpipes. It's also common to see people eating haggis, drinking Scotch whiskey and chatting together.

Cheering on the dancers is a great way to get involved and show your support for the competition. You can even get in on the action and try your hand at dancing yourself!

Dancing is a big part of Highland Games, with traditional and modern forms of dancing taking place at the same time. Some of these events feature the World Highland Dancing Championships, which bring dancers from all over the world.

Other traditional events that you'll likely see at these gatherings include caber toss, hammer throw and shot put. The caber toss involves throwing a full-length log, called a caber, into the air using both hands.

A hammer throw is similar, but the hammer is spun in circles and then thrown as far as possible. Another favorite is weight for height, where competitors toss a heavy object over a bar.

Cheer on the band.

Highland Games are a traditional Scottish gathering where families and clans meet to compete in a variety of athletic and cultural events. In addition to the athletics, attendees may enjoy food, dance, bagpipe music and even whisky tasting.

The bands can include musicians from the local community, as well as nationally renowned groups. This is one of the most fun and memorable parts of any Highland Games event.

Other common Highland Games musical activities are bagpipe competitions and solo piping and drumming events. At some Highland Games, the local chiefs will lead their members to the arena for a ceremony before they begin their competitions.

These events are known as the Heavy Events, and they are considered the heart of the games. They are composed of eight different events that test strength and power. These include the Sheaf Toss, Caber Toss, Stone Put, Hammer Throw, Light Weight Throw, Heavy Weight Throw, and Weight for Height.

Athletes must be able to carry and handle these large weights and equipment safely in order to win a prize. These events are typically only open to adult men, women and youths.

The caber toss is a famous event in the Highland Games and is a good indicator of an athlete's strength. This event sees competitors hold a 5.94m (19ft 6in) tapered pole made from wood and toss it as straight as possible.

This can be difficult for beginners and is a good way to measure an athlete's stability as they balance the caber in their hands. They must also execute a run-up before they throw it and try to make it as far as possible without hitting anything.

Cheer on the crowd.

When you attend a Highland Games event, it's easy to get caught up in the festivities. You'll find lots of food, dancing and live music. But if you want to truly experience the games, you have to look beyond the crowd and into the athletes, dancers and bands.

Many of the traditional Highland Games events are centered around strength and athletics, and some have become iconic. The most famous of these, the "caber toss," involves tossing a log called a caber (Gaelic for a wood beam) that's 19ft 6in tall and weighs around 79kg (175lbs).

Tossing a caber is considered a test of balance and control. A perfect throw sees the small end of the log aimed away from the thrower, at a '12 o'clock' angle.

Other heavy-duty contests include the hammer throw and the stone put. The hammer throw involves swinging a 22lb metal ball around the competitor's head, while the stone put requires the competitor to throw a large stone (around 20-26lb in weight) after a short run or from a standing position.

When the Phoenix Highland Games, for instance, are held in the first weekend of March, the weather is usually quite nice. Despite the setback, there are still plenty of Highland Games events happening in Arizona and Central Florida. The 45th Central Florida Scottish Games are back in Winter Springs, and the National History Museum of Central Florida is hosting a series of Virtual Events to celebrate these events in new ways.

Best restaurants, bars and clubs in Scotland

Best Restaurants in Scotland:

The Kitchin - Edinburgh: This Michelin-starred restaurant serves contemporary Scottish cuisine with an emphasis on local, seasonal produce.

The Gannet - Glasgow: This award-winning restaurant is known for its inventive Scottish cuisine, with a focus on seafood.

Ondine - Edinburgh: Another seafood-focused restaurant, Ondine is renowned for its fresh, sustainable catches and creative dishes.

The Peat Inn - St. Andrews: This elegant restaurant in a charming 18th-century inn serves refined, modern Scottish cuisine.

The Three Chimneys - Isle of Skye: Located on the stunning Isle of Skye, this restaurant is renowned for its use of local, seasonal ingredients and exceptional seafood.

Best Bars in Scotland:

The Pot Still - Glasgow: This traditional Scottish pub is known for its extensive whisky selection, with over 700 different bottles on offer.

The Finnieston - Glasgow: This trendy bar in the West End of Glasgow is known for its excellent seafood and extensive gin selection.

Bon Vivant - Edinburgh: This stylish bar and restaurant is known for its creative cocktails and refined Scottish cuisine.

Best Clubs in Scotland:

Sub Club - Glasgow: This legendary nightclub has been a mainstay of Glasgow's club scene for over 30 years, with a focus on techno and electronic music.

Sneaky Pete's - Edinburgh: This intimate club is known for its diverse line-up of live music and DJ sets, with a focus on underground and electronic music.

La Cheetah Club - Glasgow: This intimate basement club is known for its eclectic line-up of DJs and underground electronic music.

Cabaret Voltaire - Edinburgh: This stylish club in the heart of Edinburgh's Old Town hosts a variety of live music events and DJ sets, with a focus on dance and electronic music.

Chapter 5.

Tips for avoiding crowds and skipping lines

Scotland is a popular tourist destination, especially during peak seasons, which means that crowds and long lines can be expected at many popular attractions. However, there are a few tips you can follow to avoid crowds and skip lines during your trip to Scotland:

- Plan your visit during the offseason: Avoid visiting Scotland during the peak season, which is from June to August. Instead, plan your visit during the offseason, which is from November to March. During this time, you will find fewer crowds, lower prices, and shorter lines.

- Book tickets in advance: If you plan on visiting popular attractions, it's best to book your tickets in advance. Many attractions in Scotland offer online booking, which can help you avoid long lines at the ticket counter.

- Visit early in the morning or late in the afternoon: If you can't book your tickets in advance, try to visit popular attractions early in the morning or late in the afternoon when the crowds are smaller.
- Explore lesser-known attractions: Instead of visiting the most popular tourist spots, try exploring some of Scotland's lesser-known attractions. These places are often less crowded and offer a more authentic experience.
- Take a guided tour: A guided tour can help you skip lines and avoid crowds at popular attractions. Many tour companies offer skip-the-line access, which can save you a lot of time.
- Visit shopping areas: Many popular tourist attractions are located near shopping areas. If you want to avoid crowds and lines, plan your visit during a weekday instead of the weekend.
- Visit in the fall: During this time of year, many hotels and restaurants close for the season. However, you can still enjoy Scotland's beautiful weather without being surrounded by tourists.
- Go off the beaten path: Instead of visiting popular spots, try exploring less-traveled locations. You'll be able to have a more authentic experience without fighting through huge crowds and waiting in long lines.
- Visit smaller museums: If you want to avoid large crowds, visit smaller museums outside of the city center. These places are often less crowded and offer a more intimate experience.
- Eat at restaurants outside the city center: If you're looking for somewhere to eat, try exploring restaurants outside the city center. These places are often less expensive than restaurants in popular

tourist areas and offer more authentic Scottish cuisine.

Tips on places to stay

If you are looking for a cheap hotel stay there are several things that you can do to get the best value for your money. One of the main factors to consider is the location of a hotel. The closer to public transport, airports, local attractions, restaurants, beaches and parks it is the better off you will be.

Some hotels and B &B to stay

- The Witchery by the Castle - This luxurious hotel in Edinburgh is located near the famous Edinburgh Castle and offers guests a unique and historical experience.
- The Balmoral Hotel - Also located in Edinburgh, The Balmoral Hotel is a prestigious 5-star hotel with stunning views of the city and Edinburgh Castle.
- The Torridon - Situated in the Scottish Highlands, The Torridon is a beautiful country house hotel that

offers a variety of outdoor activities such as hiking, fishing, and wildlife watching.

- The Isle of Eriska Hotel - This luxurious hotel is located on a private island near Oban and is surrounded by stunning natural scenery. Guests can enjoy a variety of outdoor activities and fine dining during their stay.
- The Caledonian Hotel - Located in the heart of Glasgow, The Caledonian Hotel is a luxurious 5-star hotel that offers guests a stylish and contemporary experience.
- The Dunstane Houses - This boutique hotel in Edinburgh is located in the charming West End neighborhood and offers guests a unique and stylish experience.
- The Sherbrooke Castle Hotel - This stunning 4-star hotel is located in the south side of Glasgow and is housed in a beautifully restored Victorian mansion.
- The Glenmorangie House - Located in the Scottish Highlands, The Glenmorangie House is a charming and luxurious hotel that offers guests the opportunity to sample some of Scotland's finest whiskies.

These are just a few examples of the many great hotels and B&Bs that Scotland has to offer. When choosing where to stay in Scotland, consider your budget, location, and preferred style of accommodation to find the perfect fit for your needs.

1. Stay away from prime locations

If you are looking to save a few bucks and still enjoy a trip of a lifetime, there is no need to compromise on luxury. While you may have to put up with a mediocre room or two, there are plenty of options out there that will tick all the boxes when it comes to luxury hotels. The best of the bunch are ones that are a bit off the beaten path, but will still give you all the bang for your buck in the hotel department. In particular, there are a few places to check out in the Manhattan area of NYC, including Midtown Manhattan and Downtown Brooklyn.

2. Look for deals

If you are looking for ways to stay in luxury hotels on a budget, there are a few things you can do. For one, you can look for deals on third-party travel websites. Many offer packages that bundle flights and hotels together so you can save a lot of money on your trip. Some hotels also offer discounts during certain holidays, so you should always be on the lookout for these offers.

Another way to get great deals on hotels is by signing up for their newsletters and emails. Often, luxury hotels will send newsletters and email promotions about special events and deals they are running. By signing up to their mailing lists, you can keep up with all of the latest offers and promotions that they are offering and you may be able to grab them before others.

If you don't have the time to search for all of these deals on your own, you can hire a travel consultant to help you out. These professionals can help you find the best deals and give you the guidance you need to plan your vacation without breaking the bank. They are experts in finding deals on luxury hotels and can help you make the most of your money while traveling.

3. Book on arrival

There are many ways to get a cheaper option to a luxury hotel. You can book with a travel agency or pay in points, for example. It's also important to avoid peak travel times, so look for deals during the off-peak season.

Booking on arrival can be a great way to save money and get the best deal possible. Some hotels offer exclusive deals to guests who book through them. These can include a $100 hotel credit, plus room upgrades and other perks. These are usually worth the extra cost, as you can use them to enhance your stay.

Another benefit of booking on arrival is that you can ask for a specific room type that you might be interested in. These can be ideal if you have children or you're looking for a suite. You can also request a pool or Spa that may not be available online.

Using the hotel car for your arrival can also help you get additional perks, such as an upgrade or waiver of a late check-out charge. The driver will be familiar with the hotel and can answer any questions you might have about the property. However, Naderkhani says that it's not a requirement for luxury hotels to include these benefits in their package deals.This is why it's crucial that they provide high-quality customer service and cater to their needs. They should also be aware of their target market, so they can offer a better product/service and increase their revenue.

4. Stay outside the city centre

The best place to stay cheaper options to luxury hotels are often found outside of the city centre. For instance, if you are looking for a five-star hotel in Copenhagen, the best bet is to look beyond the tourist hubbub and book yourself into one of the many boutique properties that have set up shop in this quaint city. Not only are these properties cheaper than the traditional big boys but they also offer many of the same amenities and perks as their more expensive counterparts. This will be a great way to recoup your hard earned cash and make the most of your stay in this Nordic gem.

5. Stay in the countryside

Whether you're looking for a weekend away from the city, a long holiday or a week of blissful tranquility, the UK countryside has got something to offer everyone. With rolling hills, quaint cobblestone streets and babbling brooks to explore, the countryside is a perfect place for a secluded getaway.

A luxury countryside hotel is a retreat where you can hunker down, unwind and recharge. It should be quiet and serene, but also provide all the amenities you need to feel at home.

Some luxury countryside hotels even have their own vineyards and artisanal markets where you can find a selection of fresh local products. For example, at Chewton Glen in Hampshire, guests can take a tour of the winery and sample its delicious wines.

You can also book wellness treatments at the spa and enjoy a massage or a hot tub. A stay at an elite countryside hotel is a pleasurable experience that you'll want to repeat time and time again.

Activities to do as a family and things you can do for free in Scotland

Scotland is a beautiful country with stunning landscapes, rich history, and a vibrant culture. It offers a range of activities that can be enjoyed by families without breaking the bank. Here are some suggestions for free activities to do with your family in Scotland:

- Go on a nature walk or hike: Scotland is known for its breathtaking landscapes, and there are many trails and parks that you can explore with your family. Some popular options include Loch Lomond & The Trossachs National Park, Cairngorms National Park, and the Pentland Hills.
- Visit museums and galleries: Many museums and galleries in Scotland offer free admission. Some of the most popular ones include the National Museum of Scotland, the Kelvingrove Art Gallery and Museum, and the Scottish National Gallery.
- Explore the beaches: Scotland has some of the most beautiful beaches in the world, and many of them are free to visit. Some popular options include Luskentyre Beach, West Sands Beach, and St Andrews Beach.
- Take a historical tour: Scotland is steeped in history, and there are many historical sites and buildings that you can explore with your family. Some popular options include Edinburgh Castle, Stirling Castle, and Culloden Battlefield.
- Attend a festival or event: Scotland is famous for its festivals and events, many of which are free to attend. Some popular options include the Edinburgh Fringe Festival, the Royal Edinburgh Military Tattoo, and the Glasgow International Comedy Festival.
- Go on a wildlife watching trip: Scotland is home to a variety of wildlife, including red deer, otters, and eagles. There are many wildlife watching trips that you can take with your family, such as a boat trip to see dolphins or a guided tour of a nature reserve.

- Visit free attractions: There are many free attractions in Scotland, such as the Scottish Parliament Building, the Glasgow Necropolis, and the Falkirk Wheel.

In summary, Scotland has a lot to offer for families looking for free activities. From exploring nature, visiting museums, to enjoying festivals and events, there is something for everyone.

Transportation, buses and cabs

In Scotland, transportation buses and cabs play an essential role in connecting people and communities.

Buses:

Buses are a popular mode of transportation in Scotland, providing a cheap and efficient way to travel both within cities and between different towns and regions. The main bus operators in Scotland are Stagecoach, First Bus, and National Express. Buses usually run on a fixed route, and passengers can pay either with cash or contactless card.

In recent years, there has been an increased focus on making bus travel more sustainable, with many operators investing in hybrid or electric buses. In addition, there are also local bus services that run on demand, providing more flexibility for passengers.

Buses are an essential mode of transport in Scotland, connecting people across the country to their workplaces, schools, and other destinations. The bus network in Scotland is extensive, with a range of operators offering services across the country.

One of the most significant operators in Scotland is Stagecoach, which provides services in cities such as Aberdeen, Edinburgh, Glasgow, and Inverness. Other operators include First Bus and National Express, which offer intercity services between different towns and cities.

One of the advantages of using buses in Scotland is that they are often more affordable than other modes of transport, such as trains or taxis. Many bus operators offer discounted fares for students, children, and senior citizens, as well as discounted passes for regular commuters.

Buses in Scotland are generally reliable, with services running frequently throughout the day. Many services also offer free Wi-Fi, making it easy for passengers to stay connected while they travel.

Another advantage of using buses in Scotland is that they provide a more environmentally friendly mode of transport compared to private cars. Buses produce fewer emissions per person, making them a more sustainable option for those who want to reduce their carbon footprint.

Subway

It is a circular subway system that runs through the heart of the city, connecting key locations such as the city centre, the West End, and the South Side.

The Glasgow Subway is one of the oldest underground rail systems in the world, having been in operation since 1896. It is also one of the smallest, with just 15 stations and a total track length of 10.5 km. Despite its small size, the subway remains an essential part of Glasgow's public transport system, with over 12 million passengers using it each year.

The subway operates seven days a week, with trains running every four minutes during peak times and every six minutes at other times. The first train of the day departs at 6.30 am, and the last train of the day departs at 11.30 pm.

The Glasgow Subway uses a unique system of two-car trains, which are manually operated by a driver. The trains run in a clockwise and anticlockwise direction, with the two routes intersecting at four stations. The subway is fully accessible, with lifts and escalators providing access to all stations.

One of the main advantages of the Glasgow Subway is its convenience, with all stations located within easy walking distance of major attractions, shops, and restaurants. It also offers a fast and efficient way to travel around the city centre, especially during rush hour when traffic can be heavy.

The Glasgow Subway is a unique and essential part of Glasgow's public transport system. With its circular route, convenient location, and efficient service, it provides an easy and affordable way to travel around the city centre.

Cabs:

Cabs in Scotland are primarily operated by private hire companies and are regulated by local councils. In order to operate, taxi drivers must obtain a license, which involves passing a knowledge and skills test.

In Scotland, there are two types of taxis: hackney cabs and private hire cabs. Hackney cabs are the traditional black cabs, which can be hailed from the street or picked up from a designated taxi rank.

Both types of cabs are regulated by the council and must comply with certain standards, including having a taximeter installed and displaying the taxi license number prominently.

Overall, transportation buses and cabs are essential parts of the Scottish transport network, providing affordable and convenient options for getting around.

What to pack and different seasons to travel to Scotland

Traveling to Scotland can be tricky because of the wildly unpredictable weather. It can rain, wind, and shine - all in the same day!

It's important to pack the right clothes for your trip. Depending on the season, you'll want to bring different jackets and shoes for each type of activity.

Spring

While summer is typically considered the peak tourism season, the shoulder season is also a good time to travel to Scotland. You'll enjoy pleasant weather, fewer crowds, and cheaper airfares.

If you're planning a trip to Scotland during the shoulder season, be sure to pack light, comfortable clothing that will keep you warm without weighing you down. This includes layers of pants, t-shirts, shirts, and long skirts, as well as waterproof jackets, boots, and sturdy walking or hiking shoes that will keep you dry in case the weather is damp.

It's also a good idea to bring binoculars or a pair of telescopes, if you're looking to sightsee over long distances and admire a beautiful landscape. You may even spot wildlife including puffins, eagles, and ospreys.

The spring shoulder season is a great time to travel to Scotland as many attractions will still be open but will be less crowded than during the summer and festival seasons. You'll also save money on accommodations and car rentals, so it's a great time to plan an affordable getaway!

For wildlife lovers, this is the perfect time to see ospreys in Cairngorms National Park and seabirds along Scotland's west coast. In addition, the country's higher peaks will be covered with snow, making it a lovely time to hike to the top.

If you are traveling to Scotland during this season, be sure to bring insect repellent. It's especially important if you're planning to hike in the Highlands where there are tons of bugs and midges.

You'll also want to have a waterproof camera bag or pouch, raincoat, and umbrella. You should also bring a lightweight wool sweater, thermal underwear, and hat or gloves to protect yourself from the cold.

If you're planning to visit Scotland during the winter, consider packing a blanket scarf as well. This can be used as a blanket on the plane, train, or bus and is a great way to stay warm.

Summer

A trip to Scotland can be a great adventure. Its scenery is breathtaking and there are many different things to do. However, the weather can be tricky and a little bit frustrating at times so you want to ensure you pack correctly.

The most important thing to remember is that Scotland has a temperate climate, so you'll need to be prepared for varying temperatures throughout the year. If you plan to do some outdoor activities, you should also bring a pair of hiking shoes as it can get very cold in the mountains.

For a day trip to Edinburgh or Glasgow, I would recommend packing nice jeans, chinos or trousers and a nice shirt, along with good comfortable boots/shoes that can be waterproofed. You will most likely be walking on cobblestones or skinny sidewalks, so make sure your footwear is comfortable and easy to navigate.

In the summer, you should also pack a sun hat and sunglasses to protect yourself from UV rays. You should also pack a pair of lightweight long-sleeved t-shirts, along with a light weight woollen sweater or cashmere jumper to wear underneath your clothes.

Another important thing to remember is that you will need to pack a rain coat and a waterproof umbrella. It can be very windy and it's a common occurrence to have rain during the summer, so make sure you have enough to keep yourself dry and protected from the elements!

You should also bring a hat, gloves and a moisture-wicking scarf to help you stay warm during the day. A hat will prevent you from getting too hot while walking and will help keep your face from overheating as well.

I would also highly recommend bringing a water-resistant daypack to carry your essentials on trips and excursions outside of the city. The rain in Scotland can be very hard on fragile electronics and other sensitive items, so a daypack will help you keep your valuables safe.

Fall

There is something so special about Scotland in the fall, and autumn foliage in particular is a must-see when you visit. The trees come alive with vibrant colors of yellow, red and orange, creating a photographer's dream. You can also find amazing waterfalls at their peak flow, and the cooler temperatures can drive away the infamous midges that tend to plague the area in the summer.

When traveling to Scotland in the fall, make sure to pack thermals, a windproof jacket and a waterproof coat. These layers will keep you comfortable no matter the weather.

One of the best places to visit in autumn is the Cairngorms National Park, where the evergreen fir trees turn brightly colored with golden hues and the mountains are covered in stunning moss. This park is also home to more than twenty lochs, each with a stunning view and a chance to enjoy nature in all its glory.

Another great place to go in Scotland in the fall is Loch Lomond, where the lochs come alive with autumn colours of shocking red, orange and yellow. The falls in this loch are also at their best, and you can walk across the path above them for great views of the waterfalls.

You'll see a lot of deer in autumn, and this is the time to watch their rut battles. In addition, wild salmon are jumping up the rivers to spawn and grey seal pups are born along the west coast.

If you're a wildlife lover, this is the perfect time of year to spot ptarmigans, red squirrels and mountain hares. If you're lucky, you may even be able to spot the elusive peregrine falcon.

In addition, autumn is a great time of year to explore ruins, castles and museums. Unlike during the summer, there is usually less crowding and you can enjoy more intimate tours. You'll also be able to enjoy more of the local cuisine and experience Scottish culture in a relaxed manner.

Winter

Scotland is a country that can get a little cold during certain seasons, so it's important to pack appropriately. If you're planning to visit in the winter, be sure to pack a warm sweater or coat, thermal underwear, wool socks and a pair of waterproof boots.

Depending on where you're staying, it may be hard to find power outlets in the Scottish countryside, so bring a universal adapter. Having an outlet with you is essential for charging your phone, camera and other gadgets.

If you're going on a hike, make sure to pack some insect repellent, as it's not uncommon for gnats or other insects to bite tourists while hiking around bodies of water, such as rivers and lakes.

The Scottish weather can be a bit unpredictable, especially in autumn, so be prepared for rainy days and chilly nights. Be sure to pack a lightweight coat and a pair of boots with good grips, a hat and a warm scarf to keep you dry.

It's also a good idea to bring an umbrella, though this isn't always necessary, and you can usually use your waterproof jacket instead. In any case, be prepared for the worst of it and have a plan B in place.

For the best time of year to travel to Scotland, try shoulder season (May, early June, September, and early October). During these months, prices are lower than in summer, but you'll still enjoy smaller crowds, better room availability, and most tourist attractions.

If you plan to travel in the winter, be aware that some museums, galleries and castles close for the season. However, some are open all year long and there's no reason you can't enjoy your trip to Scotland even in the darkest months!

Despite the fact that it is often raining or snowing in Scotland, you can still see some spectacular scenery. There's plenty to see in the Highlands and Islands, so be prepared to enjoy some outdoor adventures in the winter.

If you're road tripping through the Scottish Highlands, you'll need to have your travel maps pre-programmed on your smart phone before leaving home. This will ensure you know exactly where you're going, without having to look at an app or worry about getting lost.

Scottish slang phraseology

Scottish slang phraseology can vary greatly depending on the region and dialect. Here are some Scottish slang words and phrases that might be useful for travelers to Scotland:

- Hello - In Scotland, you might hear people use the word "hiya" or "hullo" instead of "hello." It's a friendly and informal way of greeting someone.
- Good morning - A common Scottish greeting in the morning is "mornin'" or "guid mornin'."
- Where is this place? - If you're lost or trying to find a particular location, you could ask someone "whaur's this place?" or "whaur's (name of location)?"
- Thank you - In Scotland, you might hear people say "cheers" instead of "thank you." It's a casual way of expressing gratitude.
- Aye - This is a word that means "yes" in Scotland. It's pronounced like "eye."
- Wee - As mentioned before, "wee" is a word that means small or little. You might hear someone say "a wee bit further" if you ask for directions.
- Ta - "Ta" is another slang term for "thank you" in Scotland. It's a shortened version of "thanks a lot."
- Bonnie - If you want to compliment someone or something in Scotland, you could use the word "bonnie," which means beautiful or pretty.
- Ken - As mentioned before, "ken" is a word that means to know or understand. If you don't understand something, you could say "I dinnae ken."
- Slàinte mhath - This is a traditional Scottish toast that means "good health." You might hear it being used during a meal or when raising a glass with friends.

Learning a few Scottish slang words and phrases can help you better understand the local culture and communicate with the locals on your trip to Scotland.

Chapter 6.

Tips on currency exchange

If you're planning a trip to Scotland and need to exchange currency, there are several tips that can help you get the most out of your exchange:

- Research exchange rates: Before you exchange currency, research the exchange rates to get an idea of how much you can expect to receive for your money. It's important to keep in mind that exchange rates can vary from day to day, so be sure to check them again closer to your trip.

- Avoid exchanging at airports or tourist areas: Exchange rates at airports or tourist areas are often less favorable, so it's best to avoid exchanging money in these locations if possible. Instead, look for banks or currency exchange offices in the city or town you're visiting.

- Use credit cards for large purchases: If you need to make a large purchase, such as a hotel room or a rental car, consider using your credit card instead of cash. Many credit cards offer favorable exchange rates and may also provide additional perks like travel insurance or cashback rewards.

- Be aware of fees: When exchanging currency, be aware of any fees that may be charged. Some currency exchange offices or banks may charge a commission or transaction fee for exchanging money. You may also be charged a fee if you withdraw cash from an ATM using a foreign debit card.

- Consider using a travel card: A travel card is a prepaid card that you can load with foreign currency before your trip. These cards often offer competitive exchange rates and may also provide additional benefits like travel insurance or fraud protection.

- Plan ahead: It's a good idea to plan ahead and exchange your currency before you arrive in Scotland. This will give you time to research exchange rates and find the best option for exchanging your money. It will also ensure that you have the local currency you need for your trip.

- Bring a mix of cash and cards: While credit cards are widely accepted in Scotland, it's always a good idea to have some cash on hand for smaller purchases or for places that may not accept cards. It's also important to note that some smaller businesses may only accept cash, so having a mix of cash and cards can be helpful.

- Be cautious with ATMs: When using an ATM to withdraw cash, be cautious of potential scams or skimming devices. Try to use ATMs that are located in well-lit and public areas, and always cover the keypad when entering your PIN.

- Consider exchanging currency in advance: If you're worried about exchange rates fluctuating or not being able to find a currency exchange office in Scotland, consider exchanging currency in advance. You can often do this at your local bank or at a currency exchange office in your home country.

- Don't exchange more than you need: It's best to only exchange the amount of money you need for your trip, as you may end up losing money if you exchange more than you need and then have to exchange it back at a less favorable rate. Be sure to also factor in any additional fees or commissions that may be charged when exchanging currency.

By following these tips, you can ensure that you get the most out of your currency exchange in Scotland and have the local currency you need for your trip.